ABT

ALLEN COUNTY

P9-ECL-229

U.S. WARS

THE COLD WAR

A MyReportLinks.com Book

R. Conrad Stein

MyReportLinks.com Books
an imprint of
Enslow Publishers, Inc. E
Box 398, 40 Industrial Road
Berkeley Heights, NJ 07922
USA

MyReportLinks.com Books, an imprint of Enslow Publishers, Inc.

Copyright © 2002 by Enslow Publishers, Inc.

All rights reserved.

No part of this book may be reproduced by any means
without the written permission of the publisher.

Library of Congress Cataloging-in-Publication Data

Stein, R. Conrad.
    The Cold War / R. Conrad Stein.
        p. cm. — (U.S. wars)
    Summary: Examines the history of the Cold War, including political,
economic, military, and athletic battles, from the Berlin Airlift of
1948 to the fall of the Berlin Wall in 1989. Includes Internet links to
Web sites, source documents, and photographs related to the war.
    Includes bibliographical references and index.
    ISBN 0-7660-5095-5
    1. Cold War—Juvenile literature. 2. United States—History—1945– —
Juvenile literature. [1. Cold War. 2. World politics—1945–1989. 3. United
States—Foreign relations—Soviet Union. 4. Soviet Union—Foreign relations—
United States.] I. Title. II. Series.
D843 .S77 2002
909.82'5—dc21
                                        2001008197

Printed in the United States of America

10 9 8 7 6 5 4 3 2 1

To Our Readers:
Through the purchase of this book, you and your library gain access to the Report Links that specifically back up this book.
The Publisher will provide access to the Report Links that back up this book and will keep these Report Links up to date on **www.myreportlinks.com** for three years from the book's first publication date.
We have done our best to make sure all Internet addresses in this book were active and appropriate when we went to press. However, the author and the Publisher have no control over, and assume no liability for, the material available on those Internet sites or on other Web sites they may link to.
The usage of the MyReportLinks.com Books Web site is subject to the terms and conditions stated on the Usage Policy Statement on **www.myreportlinks.com**.
In the future, a password may be required to access the Report Links that back up this book. The password is found on the bottom of page 4 of this book.
Any comments or suggestions can be sent by e-mail to comments@myreportlinks.com or to the address on the back cover.

Photo Credits: AP/ Wide World Photos, p. 1; © Corel Corporation, pp. 1 (background), 3; Courtesy of America's Story from America's Library, p. 41; Courtesy of CNN.com, pp. 17, 28, 36; Courtesy of Gerald R. Ford Library, p. 42; Courtesy of John Fitzgerald Kennedy Library, p. 33; Courtesy of Le Mémorial de Caen, p. 31; Courtesy of Learning Curve, p. 16; Courtesy of MyReportLinks.com Books, p. 4; Courtesy of Smithsonian National Museum of American History, pp. 23, 44; Courtesy of Space Race, National Air and Space Museum, p. 38; Courtesy of The American Experience, PBS, p. 20; Courtesy of Thinkquest Library, pp. 25, 26, 30; Courtesy of U.S. Air Forces in Europe, Berlin Airlift Web site, p. 11; Enslow Publishers, Inc., pp. 13, 24; Library of Congress, pp. 12, 19, 27.

Cover Photo: AP/ Wide World Photos

Cover Description: East German soldiers atop the Berlin Wall

Contents

MyReportLinks.com Books
Great Books, Great Links, Great for Research!

MyReportLinks.com Books present the information you need to learn about your report subject. In addition, they show you where to go on the Internet for more information. The pre-evaluated Report Links that back up this book are kept up to date on **www.myreportlinks.com**. With the purchase of a MyReportLinks.com Books title, you and your library gain access to the Report Links that specifically back up that book. The Report Links save hours of research time and link to dozens—even hundreds—of Web sites, source documents, and photos related to your report topic.

Please see "To Our Readers" on the Copyright page for important information about this book, the MyReportLinks.com Books Web site, and the Report Links that back up this book.

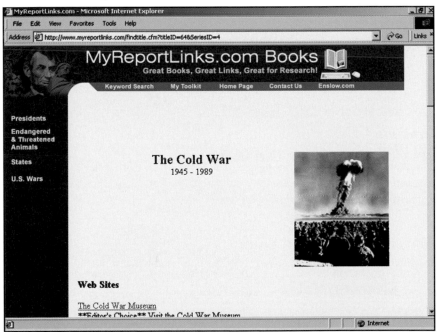

Access:

The Publisher will provide access to the Report Links that back up this book and will try to keep these Report Links up to date on our Web site for three years from the book's first publication date. Please enter **UCW7475** if asked for a password.

 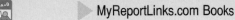

Report Links

The Internet sites described below can be accessed at
http://www.myreportlinks.com

*EDITOR'S CHOICE

▶ **The Cold War Museum**

At this site the information about the Cold War is in the format of a
time line. By clicking on each decade, you can access essays about
pivotal events and links to other sources. There is also an online
exhibition where you can find photos of the Berlin Wall.

Link to this Internet site from http://www.myreportlinks.com

*EDITOR'S CHOICE

▶ **Fast Attacks & Boomers**

At this site, you can access information about the history of submarines
in the Cold War, how nuclear submarines were built and maintained,
and what life is like aboard one.

Link to this Internet site from http://www.myreportlinks.com

*EDITOR'S CHOICE

▶ **Race for the Superbomb**

At this PBS Web site you can read about the arms race between the
Soviet Union and the United States. You will also find a biography of
Joseph Stalin, footage of actual nuclear blasts, a time line, and maps.

Link to this Internet site from http://www.myreportlinks.com

*EDITOR'S CHOICE

▶ **A Concrete Curtain: The Life and Death of the
Berlin Wall**

At this Web site you will find a detailed history of the Berlin Wall from
its creation in 1961 to its destruction in 1989. You can also explore
maps and images of the Berlin Wall.

Link to this Internet site from http://www.myreportlinks.com

*EDITOR'S CHOICE

▶ **CNN: The Cold War**

This informative site has data about technology used during the Cold
War, the history of atomic and hydrogen bombs, biographies of key
people, and many facts about espionage. You can read about tools spies
used, such as weapons disguised as cigarette cases.

Link to this Internet site from http://www.myreportlinks.com

*EDITOR'S CHOICE

▶ **President Nixon Goes to China**

America's Story from America's Library, a Library of Congress Web site,
tells the story of Nixon's famous trip to Communist China.

Link to this Internet site from http://www.myreportlinks.com

 The Internet sites described below can be accessed at
http://www.myreportlinks.com

▶ The Alger Hiss Story
In 1948, Whittaker Chambers charged that Alger Hiss had helped Chambers spy for the Soviet Union. At this Web site you can read an overview of Hiss's life and explore the court case in which Hiss was found guilty and sent to prison for forty-four months.

Link to this Internet site from http://www.myreportlinks.com

▶ The Avalon Project: The Cold War
This site has transcripts of memorandums written by the U.S. government about the Cuban Missile Crisis, the U-2 Incident, the Warsaw Security Pact, and more. You can also read the treaty that formed NATO.

Link to this Internet site from http://www.myreportlinks.com

▶ Biography of John F. Kennedy
The official White House Web site holds the biography John F. Kennedy, the president in office during the Cuban Missile Crisis. There is a link from his biography to the JFK Library and Museum, which has interesting essays such as "JFK Questioned Value of Nuclear Build-Up."

Link to this Internet site from http://www.myreportlinks.com

▶ Cold War
This Webquest Web site provides thought-provoking questions about the Cold War, the wartime relationships between Britain, the United States, and the USSR, the causes of the war, and much more.

Link to this Internet site from http://www.myreportlinks.com

▶ Cold War
This site addresses tensions between the United States and the Soviet Union, as well as the emergence of China as a Communist nation. There are also essays explaining "détente," the easing of tensions.

Link to this Internet site from http://www.myreportlinks.com

▶ The Cold War
This site has easy-to-understand material divided into four sections: the space race, arms race, world politics, and propaganda and ideology. Within each section there are time lines or biographies.

Link to this Internet site from http://www.myreportlinks.com

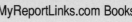
Report Links

 The Internet sites described below can be accessed at
http://www.myreportlinks.com

▶ **The Cold War, from Beginning to End**
This comprehensive site looks back at the fall of Communism, and
contains articles about the Berlin Wall, life in Russia today, and a link
to a photographic project called "Beyond the Fall."

Link to this Internet site from http://www.myreportlinks.com

▶ **For European Recovery: The Fiftieth Anniversary of the
Marshall Plan**
At this Library of Congress Web site you will learn about the history of
the Marshall Plan and about key dates in the plan's development.

Link to this Internet site from http://www.myreportlinks.com

▶ **Harry Truman: The Plain-Speaking Man of Independence**
At this site you can learn about the president who was in office during
the early years of the Cold War. There is a page devoted to Truman's
handling of foreign affairs in the Cold War era.

Link to this Internet site from http://www.myreportlinks.com

▶ **Korean War Fiftieth Anniversary**
At this site you can access images from the Korean War, interviews with
participants, and historic information. There are also links to additional
Web resources.

Link to this Internet site from http://www.myreportlinks.com

▶ **The Life and Times of Winston Churchill**
This site contains facts about Churchill, his speeches and quotes,
the history of his life, Churchill trivia, and debates about his role
as a war leader.

Link to this Internet site from http://www.myreportlinks.com

▶ **McCarthyism**
At this site you will learn about how the Cold War affected
America, with the formation of the House Committee on
Un-American Activities, and Senator Joseph McCarthy's list of
suspected Communists.

Link to this Internet site from http://www.myreportlinks.com

Back   Forward   Stop   Review   Home   Explore   Favorites   History

Report Links

 The Internet sites described below can be accessed at
http://www.myreportlinks.com

NATO Official Homepage

This official Web site of NATO lists participating countries and representatives. It has a transcription of the actual treaty, and includes photos of the signing of the treaty and more. There is a search key where you can look for information about the Cold War.

Link to this Internet site from http://www.myreportlinks.com

Newseum: The Berlin Wall

This informative site depicts the history of the Berlin Wall from both sides of the wall. Included are photographs, an essay, and an interactive quiz.

Link to this Internet site from http://www.myreportlinks.com

Nikita Khrushchev: Up From the Plenum

In 1957, *Time* magazine declared Russian leader Nikita Khrushchev Man of the Year. At this Web site you can read the article written about him.

Link to this Internet site from http://www.myreportlinks.com

Nixon's China Game

At this PBS Web site you will learn about Nixon's historic visit to China. Explore time lines of relations between the United States and China, maps, and an interview with Henry Kissinger. You will also find brief biographies of key players such as Mao Tse-Tung, Chou En-Lai, Richard M. Nixon, and Kissinger.

Link to this Internet site from http://www.myreportlinks.com

Space Race

At this interesting site, you can see pictures of satellites such as *Sputnik*, and learn about the competition to reach the moon. There is also a page about declassified paintings of Soviet space weapons.

Link to this Internet site from http://www.myreportlinks.com

Sputnik

This site has photos of *Sputnik*, the history behind the satellite, official Soviet and United States documents, a time line of events, and more.

Link to this Internet site from http://www.myreportlinks.com

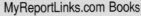
Report Links

➤ The Internet sites described below can be accessed at
http://www.myreportlinks.com

▶This Day in Cold War History
Each day this site describes a new event that occurred during the
Cold War. You can also do a search for "Cold War" to access
more information.

Link to this Internet site from http://www.myreportlinks.com

▶Time Line: Fifty Years of Communism in China
This *New York Times* Web site has a time line of Communist related
events in China for the past fifty years. You can also click on the
archives link to read newspaper reports from that event.

Link to this Internet site from http://www.myreportlinks.com

▶USAFE Berlin Airlift Site
This site contains historic information, a time line, video clips, photos,
and biographies of key players in the Berlin Airlift.

Link to this Internet site from http://www.myreportlinks.com

▶Vice President Johnson Was Assigned the Task of Unifying the U.S. Satellite Programs
The launching of *Sputnik* prompted President Kennedy to assign Vice
President Lyndon B. Johnson the task of bringing together the United
States satellite programs.

Link to this Internet site from http://www.myreportlinks.com

▶Winston Churchill
This site has a transcription of Churchill's speech, in which he states
that an iron curtain has descended across the Continent.

Link to this Internet site from http://www.myreportlinks.com

▶Fourteen Days in October
This information packed site has a thorough breakdown of all the
events that happened before, during, and after the Cuban Missile
Crisis. You will also find biographies of the key players, pictures,
an interactive quiz, and more.

Link to this Internet site from http://www.myreportlinks.com

Cold War Time Line

1945—*Feb. 4–11:* United States and Allied leaders decide to divide postwar Germany.

    —*May 7:* Germany surrenders, ending World War II in Europe.

1946—*March 5:* Winston Churchill makes "Iron Curtain" speech.

1947—*June:* U.S. Secretary of State George Marshall proposes aid for European nations willing to resist Communism. This becomes known as the Marshall Plan.

1948—*June 24:* The Soviet Union closes all entrances to Berlin.

1949—*April 4:* United States and its allies form military alliance, NATO.

    —*Aug. 29:* The Soviet Union tests its first atomic bomb.

    —*Oct. 1:* China establishes a Communist government.

1950—*June 25:* North Korea invades South Korea, starting the Korean War.

1952—*Nov. 1:* The United States tests its first hydrogen bomb.

1953—*Aug. 20:* The Soviet Union tests its first hydrogen bomb.

1955—*May 14:* Warsaw Pact is established.

1956—*Oct.:* Anti-Communist revolt in Hungary is crushed.

1957—*Oct. 4:* Soviet Union launches *Sputnik*; space race begins.

1960—*May 1:* American U-2 spy plane shot down over Soviet territory.

1961—*Aug.:* East Germany builds Berlin Wall.

1962—*Oct.:* Soviet missiles discovered in Cuba.

1963—*July:* United States, Great Britain, and Soviet Union end nuclear tests in the atmosphere.

1972—*Feb. 21:* President Nixon begins visit to China.

1987—*Dec. 8:* President Ronald Reagan and Soviet General Secretary Mikhail Gorbachev sign the INF Treaty.

1989—*Aug.:* Non-Communists gain office in Poland.

    —*Nov.:* Jubilant crowds tear down Berlin Wall.

1990—*Oct. 3:* Germany is reunited.

1991—The Soviet Union collapses.

Drama in the Skies

Only a few buildings stood undamaged in Berlin in the summer of 1948. Roofless shells of apartments and office buildings lined the streets. Three years earlier, Berlin was destroyed by bombs and gunfire in a savage battle. Now Berlin and its struggling residents faced another battle in a new war—the Cold War. This new conflict emerged from the ashes of World War II.

Berlin Airlift Photo Gallery - Microsoft Internet Explorer

File   Edit   View   Favorites   Tools   Help

Address http://www.usafe.af.mil/berlin/photos2.htm

Goods bound for Berlin being loaded on a C-47 "Skytrain" in April 1949.

Workers outside Frankfurt load flour from freight cars to trailer trucks. The flour will be taken to Rhein-Main Airfield for shipment to Berlin.

Done   Internet

▲ *The Berlin Airlift began in June 1948 to give support to Berlin, in order to protect it from a Communist takeover.*

Forces from the United States, Great Britain, France, and the Soviet Union now occupied Germany. Berlin was Germany's capital and its largest city, with a population of 2.5 million. Berlin lay in the zone controlled by the Soviets, yet the United States, Britain, and France also controlled a portion of the city.

On June 24, 1948, the Soviet Union, also called the USSR, closed all roads and train lines into Berlin. No one could enter or leave the city. The Communists gave no reason for these actions. One official mumbled that the train tracks were shut down "for repairs." However, the explanation for the sudden blockade was clear to the United States: The Soviets wanted to cut off Berlin's supplies and force Berliners to accept Communist rule. In Washington, D.C., U.S. President Harry Truman decided to move supplies to Berlin by plane. He would not abandon the city to the Communists. "We stay in Berlin, period," he said in June 1948.[1] It was a bold move. Nobody had ever tried to supply a major city with food and other requirements from the air.

For the next eleven months, the world watched the Berlin Airlift in action. Huge cargo planes roared in and out of the surrounded city. Sometimes Soviet fighter aircraft played a dangerous game of "chicken." The fighters raced head-on at the slow-moving cargo carriers. Then they veered off at the last second to avoid a crash.

◀ *President Harry S Truman.*

▲ *Located deep in the Soviet zone, Berlin became a target for a Communist takeover.*

The cargo planes carried food, including bread, fresh milk, and eggs. When winter began, they also brought coal so the people of Berlin could heat their homes. One popular American pilot dropped tiny parachutes holding candy bars. Berliners called him the "candy bomber."

At the height of the Berlin Airlift, cargo planes using Tempelhof and Gatow airports landed and took off at the rate of one every ninety seconds. Tiny Gatow became the world's busiest airport. Crews flew in blinding fog and roaring winds. Crashes killed fifty-five American and British airmen. By April 1949, planes were delivering 8,000 tons of supplies to the city each day.

The Soviets ended their blockade without explanation on May 12, 1949. Americans thought the Berlin Airlift was a major victory over Communism. Historians now call the airlift the first battle of the Cold War—a conflict that gripped the world for almost fifty years.

The Seeds of War

On the morning of April 25, 1945, a unit of thirty-five American soldiers approached the Elbe River in central Germany. Europe had been at war for more than five years. The troops were tense. A lieutenant peered across the Elbe through binoculars and saw soldiers wearing brown shirts. Germans? No, these men were Soviets. The Americans splashed through the river and saluted the Soviets in proper military fashion. The men hugged and danced with each other. The Americans and the Soviets—allies throughout World War II—had met on their enemy's soil. The struggle in Europe was nearly over.

▶ An Ending and a Beginning

World War II was a devastating conflict. Some 55 million people died during six years of war. The war ended officially on September 2, 1945, when Japan surrendered to the United States and its allies. The fighting stopped—but the seeds of a new war were growing.

In February 1945, leaders of the United States, Great Britain, and the Soviet Union met at the city of Yalta on the Black Sea. They were close to victory over Germany, and these "Big Three" wanted to make plans for the future. The leaders agreed that the Soviets would take control of the eastern half of Germany. The Americans and their allies would look after the western half. This division of Germany was expected to be temporary.

The Big Three met again in July 1945 in the German city of Potsdam. The Americans and British were uneasy

Back   Forward   Stop   Review   Home   Explore   Favorites   History

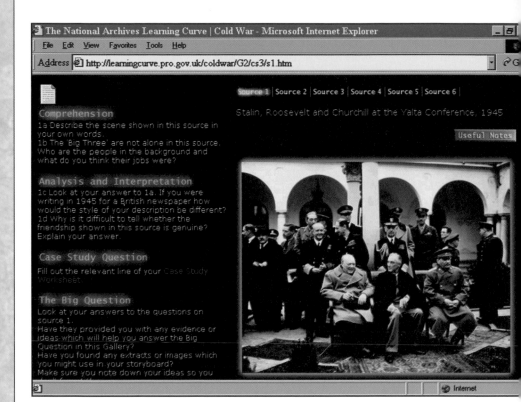

The National Archives Learning Curve | Cold War - Microsoft Internet Explorer

File Edit View Favorites Tools Help

Address http://learningcurve.pro.gov.uk/coldwar/G2/cs3/s1.htm

Source 1 | Source 2 | Source 3 | Source 4 | Source 5 | Source 6 |

Stalin, Roosevelt and Churchill at the Yalta Conference, 1945

Useful Notes

Comprehension
1a Describe the scene shown in this source in your own words.
1b The 'Big Three' are not alone in this source. Who are the people in the background and what do you think their jobs were?

Analysis and Interpretation
1c Look at your answer to 1a. If you were writing in 1945 for a British newspaper how would the style of your description be different?
1d Why is it difficult to tell whether the friendship shown in this source is genuine? Explain your answer.

Case Study Question
Fill out the relevant line of your Case Study Worksheet.

The Big Question
Look at your answers to the questions on source 1.
Have they provided you with any evidence or ideas which will help you answer the Big Question in this Gallery?
Have you found any extracts or images which you might use in your storyboard?
Make sure you note down your ideas so you

Internet

In February 1945, Churchill, Roosevelt, and Stalin (pictured left to right), met at the Yalta Conference to discuss the future of Germany.

about the USSR's actions. Soviet troops and tanks were stationed in Poland, Romania, Bulgaria, Czechoslovakia, and Hungary. The Americans and the British believed the Russians—who headed the mighty Soviet Union—wished to spread their Communist beliefs to these nations.

The Cold War—a struggle between those who believed in Communism and those who opposed it—had no dramatic beginning. Many historians trace the actual start of the war to a speech by British leader Winston Churchill. In Fulton, Missouri, on March 5, 1946, Churchill said of Europe, "From Stettin in the Baltic to Trieste in the Adriatic, an iron curtain has descended across the

Continent."[1] Soon journalists in the United States and Western Europe called Eastern European nations the "Iron Curtain countries." A popular American newspaper writer, Walter Lippmann, was the first to use the phrase "Cold War."

A Look at Communism

The word *communism* comes from a Latin root meaning "belonging to all." A true Communist believes that the citizens of a nation should share the nation's wealth—its farms, factories, ships, and mines. Individuals should not be allowed to have their own private money (capital). Communism, therefore, is the opposite of *capitalism*, the

▲ Winston Churchill used the phrase "Iron Curtain" in March 1946. This map shows which Eastern European countries lay behind the Iron Curtain.

economic system of the United States and many other countries around the world.

Karl Marx described the basic principles of Communism in *The Communist Manifesto* in 1848. Marx said that world peace would be possible when all the nations were Communist. He also said that rich capitalists would never choose to give up their lifestyle. The workers would have to take control by force. Many Americans believed that all Communists were dangerous. Communists threatened the American way of life, they thought.

In 1917, Russian workers and peasants rebelled against their leaders and established a Communist government. The world was stunned. However, the new Soviet government did not create the promised paradise for workers. Instead, the government imprisoned and executed many who opposed them.

New Alliances

Conditions in war-weary Europe were ideal for Communist governments to take advantage of countries that had been weakened. There were no jobs, people were hungry, and their clothes were tattered. The Communists promised a new, fairer system for all.

In 1946, Communists in Greece rebelled against their government. President Harry Truman wanted to help the Greek people resist Communism. He approved $400 million in aid to help rebuild Greece and to provide jobs. His belief that the United States should help nations struggling against Communism became known as the Truman Doctrine.

A rebuilding program called the Marshall Plan was launched in 1948. Under this plan the United States sent

$13 billion in food, seeds, farm machinery, and industrial products to Europe. The plan was named for its creator, U.S. Secretary of State George Marshall. Funds from the Marshall Plan poured into Europe until 1951.

Western European nations received most of this aid. Poland and Czechoslovakia asked to be included, but the Soviet Union refused to allow them to participate. The Soviet army had powerful military units stationed in Eastern Europe. These countries were forced to obey the wishes of the Soviet leaders.

New military alliances were formed during the postwar period. In April 1949, the North Atlantic Treaty Organization (NATO) was established. The original members of NATO were Belgium, Canada, Denmark, France, Great Britain, Iceland, Italy, Luxembourg, the Netherlands, Norway, Portugal, and the United States. Greece and Turkey became NATO members in 1952. West Germany joined the alliance in 1955.

The Communist nations of Eastern Europe formed their own military alliance, known as the Warsaw Pact, in 1955. Nations in the Warsaw Pact included Albania, Bulgaria, Czechoslovakia, East Germany, Hungary, Poland, and Romania. The Soviet Union led the Warsaw Pact, and its headquarters were in Moscow.

The two alliances were based on similar agreements. If an

Vladimir Lenin founded the ▶ Communist Party in Russia.

enemy attacked any member of the alliance, all nations in that alliance would go to war. An attack on one member meant an attack on all.

Thus two opposing sides developed in postwar Europe. The Soviet Union headed what was called the Eastern Bloc. The United States, Great Britain, and France led the Western Bloc. East was against West. The Communist nations were against the capitalist nations.

▶ Struggles in China

Communist and Nationalist forces had fought a long civil war in China. In 1949, the Communists, under Mao Tse-Tung, completed a takeover of that huge country. The

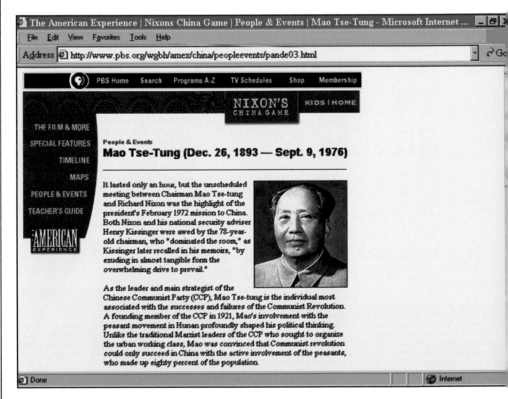

▲ Mao Tse-Tung and his Communist forces took over China in 1949.

Nationalist leaders escaped to the island of Taiwan (also known as Formosa) and formed a new country, then called Nationalist China.

Mainland China became the People's Republic of China. American newspapers often called it Red China. Red is the color associated with Communism.

With the revolution in China, the Cold War spread from Europe to Asia. Now more than one-third of the earth's surface and one-third of its people were under the Communist flag. Many Americans thought that their country was losing the Cold War.

▶ Weapon of Fear

The United States dropped the first atomic bomb on August 6, 1945, over the city of Hiroshima, Japan. It blew up in an immense ball of fire. In the blink of an eye, the bomb blast destroyed everything directly beneath it. At least eighty thousand residents of Hiroshima died that first day. Three days later the United States dropped a second atomic bomb on Nagasaki. The results were equally devastating. On August 14, the Japanese government agreed to surrender.

In September 1949, an American B-29 bomber made a routine weather survey flight between Japan and Alaska. Its flight plan took the four-engine plane close to Soviet shores. Suddenly a Geiger counter in the crew compartment began clicking. A Geiger counter is an instrument that detects traces of radioactivity in the air. This clicking indicated that the Soviet Union had recently tested an atomic bomb.

The atomic bomb helped to end World War II, but it left the world with a terrible weapon. Now two nations held this power.

Chapter 3

The 1950s: The Cold War at Home and Abroad

The thought of Communist violence scared many Americans. Others recognized that this fear itself could be dangerous. The United States should not react without careful thought, they said. It was important to remember and uphold American values, they warned. In 1946, George Kennan, an American diplomat and historian, warned that the United States should not react too harshly to the Communists. If so, the United States ran the risk of appearing to be just as dangerous and evil as the Soviet Union was thought to be.[1]

▶ "Duck and Cover"

During the late 1940s and early 1950s, many Americans believed that nuclear war could break out at any moment. Sturdy buildings were declared atomic bomb shelters. They were marked with a special yellow-and-black sign. Some families built their own shelters. Citizens were told to "duck and cover"—to cover their faces and skin—if they saw the flash of a nuclear explosion. Air-raid drills interrupted classes, and children filed into school corridors and basements. Many young people were afraid the world would end before they had a chance to grow up.

A few politicians took advantage of this atmosphere of fear. They accused some American citizens of being Communist spies or sympathizers. It is true that there were Communist spies in the United States. A few had helped Russia develop its atomic bomb. However, these

http://americanhistory.si.edu/subs/history/timeline/origins/images/civdefens.jpg - Microsoft Internet Explo...

File   Edit   View   Favorites   Tools   Help

Address   http://americanhistory.si.edu/subs/history/timeline/origins/images/civdefens.jpg   Go

Done   Internet

▲ *During the 1950s, bomb and fallout shelters became common in the United States. The woman in this photograph is advertising public fallout shelters and demonstrating how the government stocks the shelters with emergency supplies.*

politicians often seemed more interested in making headlines than in finding spies.

"I have here in my hand a list of 205—a list of names that were known to the Secretary of State as being members of the Communist Party and who nevertheless are still working and shaping policy in the State Department."[2] So said Senator Joseph McCarthy in February 1950. In fact, he had no list of 205 names. Or if he did, he never showed the list to the public. McCarthy regularly accused people of being Communists, but he gave little or no evidence. He once said that Edna Ferber

(author of the popular 1950 novel *Giant*) had Communist leanings. Actually, Ferber's only "crime" was to condemn racial prejudice in her books.

In 1954, Senator McCarthy said that Communists were serving in the U.S. Army. Committees were formed to investigate. The committee hearings were broadcast on television, and the cameras showed McCarthy's true nature. He was seen as a bully and his popularity declined. Other senators considered his actions disgraceful. To this day, wildly accusing others of disloyalty to the United States is called *McCarthyism*.

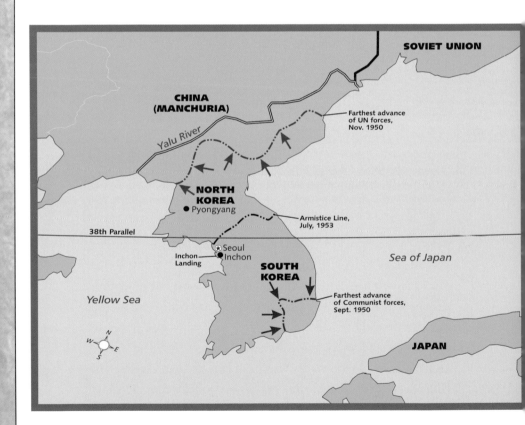

▲ In 1950, the United States entered the Korean War to protect South Korea from a Communist takeover.

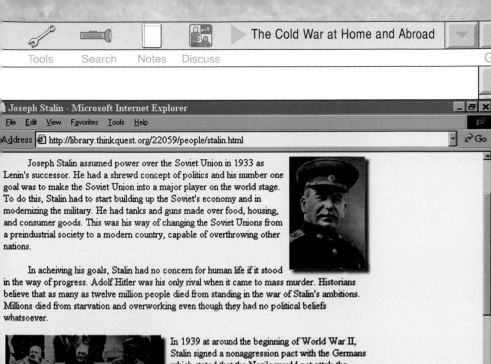

Joseph Stalin - Microsoft Internet Explorer

File Edit View Favorites Tools Help

Address http://library.thinkquest.org/22059/people/stalin.html   Go

Joseph Stalin assumed power over the Soviet Union in 1933 as Lenin's successor. He had a shrewd concept of politics and his number one goal was to make the Soviet Union into a major player on the world stage. To do this, Stalin had to start building up the Soviet's economy and in modernizing the military. He had tanks and guns made over food, housing, and consumer goods. This was his way of changing the Soviet Unions from a preindustrial society to a modern country, capable of overthrowing other nations.

In acheiving his goals, Stalin had no concern for human life if it stood in the way of progress. Adolf Hitler was his only rival when it came to mass murder. Historians believe that as many as twelve million people died from standing in the war of Stalin's ambitions. Millions died from starvation and overworking even though they had no political beliefs whatsoever.

In 1939 at around the beginning of World War II, Stalin signed a nonaggression pact with the Germans which stated that the Nazi's would not attck the Soviets and the Soviets would do the same. As a part of this deal, Poland was invaded and split up between Germany and the Soviet Union. Stalin although not liking this deal, saw that Hitler would invade the Soviet Union sometime in the future and this pact allowed him to prepare for it. Eight days after the pact was signed, Germany invaded Poland and World War

Done   Internet

▲ Joseph Stalin was a ruthless dictator who ruled the Soviet Union from 1929 until his death in 1953.

▶ Frosts and Thaws

On the morning of June 25, 1950, gunfire roared along the 38th parallel, an imaginary line that divided the country of Korea. When the guns fell silent, huge Soviet-built tanks rolled from North Korea into South Korea.

The people of Korea were also victims of the Cold War. In 1945, the peninsula nation was split in two. This division—like the division of Germany—was supposed to be temporary. However, a Communist government developed in the north and a capitalist government formed in the south. The two states became bitter enemies.

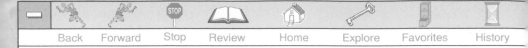

The United States sent troops to help defend South Korea. The Korean War lasted more than three years. Some 35,000 Americans died in the fighting.

Soviet Premier Joseph Stalin died on March 5, 1953. Stalin was an iron-fisted dictator who had ruled the Soviet Union since 1929. Many historians believe he ordered even more people killed than did Adolf Hitler, leader of Nazi Germany in World War II.

In 1958, Nikita Khrushchev became head of the Soviet government. Unlike Stalin, Khrushchev did not believe

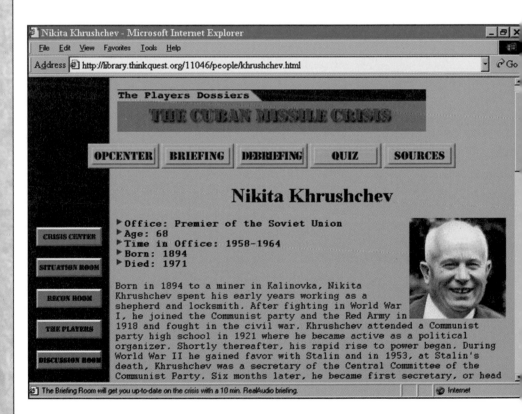

Nikita Khrushchev served as premier of the Soviet Union from 1958 until 1964. Although Premier Khrushchev had a friendly personality that many Americans enjoyed, he and President Eisenhower shared a tumultuous relationship.

that war with the West was unavoidable. The new Communist ruler had a sense of humor that Americans enjoyed. In the fall of 1959, Khrushchev came to the United States. He met with President Dwight Eisenhower at Camp David, the presidential retreat in Maryland. The talks were so friendly that reporters wrote about a "spirit of Camp David" between the two countries. However, hopes for peace did not last.

The U-2 Spy Plane

On May 1, 1960, an aircraft with long, thin wings took off from a secret base in Pakistan and headed toward the Soviet Union. The American plane was a high-flying U-2—a spy in the sky. For four years these planes had flown over the Soviet Union, photographing military sites. President Eisenhower hoped that the U-2 photographs would show how extensive the Soviet Union's weapons were. The Soviets knew about the planes but they had never been able to shoot one down. The U-2, which cruised at 70,000 feet, was too high for them. On this day, however, a Soviet rocket finally succeeded in hitting a U-2. The plane crashed and the pilot was captured. The world faced a new Cold War crisis.

American officials at first denied that the U-2 was spying over the Soviet Union. Later the

President Dwight D. Eisenhower. ▷

27

http://www.cnn.com/SPECIALS/cold.war/experience/spies/spy.gadgets/espionage/u2.lg.jpg - Microsoft Int...

File   Edit   View   Favorites   Tools   Help

Address   http://www.cnn.com/SPECIALS/cold.war/experience/spies/spy.gadgets/espionage/u2.lg.jpg

▲ In May 1960, an American U-2 spy plane, like the one pictured here, was shot down in the Soviet Union. The pilot, Francis Gary Powers, was captured by Soviet officials and confessed he was a spy.

captured pilot, Francis Gary Powers, admitted he was a spy. The U-2 Incident ruined a conference that took place two weeks after the plane was shot down. At the conference, Khrushchev shook his fists and demanded a formal apology from the United States. Eisenhower refused to apologize.

The World at the Brink

In the 1950s, the United States and the Soviet Union worked to build up stocks of nuclear weapons. The atomic bomb (also called the A-bomb) was followed by the much more powerful hydrogen bomb (also called the H-bomb). The United States tested its first H-bomb on a small Pacific island in November 1952. The blast produced a dazzling white fireball more than three miles in diameter. Scientists estimated that the H-bomb was a thousand times more powerful than the A-bomb that destroyed Hiroshima in 1945. Just nine months after the U.S. test, the Soviet Union fired its first H-bomb.

By 1960, the United States and the Soviet Union had stockpiled enough atomic and hydrogen bombs to destroy all life on earth. Each side recognized the danger. Each side was also aware that if it launched the first weapon, it would immediately be destroyed by the other side. Everyone hoped that this "balance of terror" would make nuclear war unthinkable. Some military men called the concept "Mutually Assured Destruction." They referred to it by its initials: MAD.

The arms race was not only about the weapons. The bombs had to be sent across great distances. In the 1940s and 1950s, the United States had an advantage. American bombers could reach Soviet territory from NATO airbases in Europe. Soviet bombers, on the other hand, had to cross either the Atlantic Ocean or the Pacific Ocean to reach the United States. By the late 1950s, rocket-propelled "ballistic" missiles were being developed. These could

shoot across an ocean in half an hour. Armed with nuclear tips, ballistic missiles became the sabers—the most popular weapons of the Cold War.

▶ The Berlin Wall

In June 1961, the new American president, John F. Kennedy, traveled to Europe to meet with Nikita Khrushchev. They hoped to ease tensions between East and West. The meeting had the opposite result.

The two leaders discussed the city of Berlin, which was a major subject of disagreement. The former German capital was now an island city, about 90 miles inside the

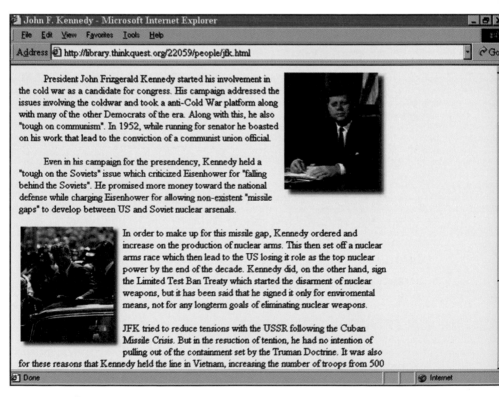

▲ The Berlin Wall was built during President John F. Kennedy's administration, despite his attempt to establish peace with Soviet Premier Nikita Khrushchev.

Berlin Wall - Microsoft Internet Explorer

File Edit View Favorites Tools Help

Address http://www.wall-berlin.org/gb/ombre.htm   Go

A CONCRETE CURTAIN
THE LIFE AND DEATH OF THE BERLIN WALL

Le Mémorial
de Caen

More and more
impassible

THE SHARED SKY
"WALL OF CHINA"
THE "WALL" SYSTEM
IN ITS SHADOW
THE FALL
WHAT IS LEFT

Internet

▲ The Berlin Wall was erected in 1961 to divide the city of Berlin into Communist and non-Communist areas. The Soviet Union built the Berlin Wall to prevent East Berliners from emigrating to the West.

borders of Communist East Germany. The city was divided into West Berlin and East Berlin. Communists governed the eastern half, while a democratic government operated in West Berlin.

At the meeting, Khrushchev demanded that the West give up West Berlin. Kennedy refused. The two leaders became angry because they could not agree. Slapping his hand on the table, Khrushchev said, "I want peace. But if you want war that is your problem." Kennedy replied coldly, "If that is true, then, Mr. Chairman, there will be war. It will be a cold winter."[1]

Fortunately for the world, the disagreement over Berlin was limited to threats and counter threats. Kennedy called up reserve army forces. Khrushchev strengthened Soviet troops. Newspaper writers called these actions "saber-rattling," which means that they were showy displays of military might. Still, no shots were fired over Berlin.

Three weeks after the Kennedy-Khrushchev meeting, the East German government put up the Berlin Wall. The purpose of the wall was to prevent East Berliners from escaping to the West. The concrete wall, topped with barbed wire, ran 102 miles through the heart of the city and out into its suburbs. Guards posted at watchtowers had orders to shoot anyone trying to climb the barrier. The Berlin Wall stood for almost thirty years, an ugly symbol of the Cold War.

▶ The Cuban Missile Crisis

In the summer of 1963, an American U-2 spy plane flew over Cuba and brought back a picture of workers clearing a soccer field on an old sugar plantation. The photo interested American intelligence agents. Cubans play baseball; Russians like soccer. More U-2 flights were ordered. Photographs from these flights revealed a startling fact: The Soviet Union was building a missile base in Cuba.

The island nation of Cuba had a troubled history. For years it was governed by a dictator named Fulgencio Batista. The United States supported Batista mainly because he was anti-Communist. On January 1, 1959, Batista was overthrown. Communist revolutionary Fidel Castro became leader of the country.

Having a Communist nation less than 100 miles from the United States made President Kennedy nervous. In

MRBM LAUNCH SITE 2
SAN CRISTOBAL
1 NOVEMBER 1962

FUEL TRAILERS

MISSILE-READY TENT

FORMER LAUNCH POSITIONS

FORMER LOCATION OF MISSILE-READY TENTS

▲ *In 1962, Cuban leader Fidel Castro began allowing the Soviet Union to place ballistic missiles in Cuba, thus sparking the Cuban Missile Crisis. This photo shows where some of the Soviet missiles in Cuba were located.*

January 1961, Kennedy approved an invasion of Cuba by Cuban exiles who were living in the United States. These anti-Castro Cubans landed at the Bay of Pigs along Cuba's south coast. Known as the Bay of Pigs Invasion, the operation was a miserable failure. Castro's forces captured most of the attackers.

Castro decided to allow the Soviets to put intermediate-range ballistic missiles on Cuba. Intermediate-range missiles can fly about 1,500 miles. Now that Khrushchev had these weapons in Cuba, he would have a better position in the military tug-of-war.

On October 22, 1962, a grim-faced President Kennedy spoke to the nation. He said that the "transformation of Cuba into an important strategic base" with "large, long-range and clearly offensive weapons" was a threat to "the peace and security of all the Americas . . . ."[2]

Kennedy announced that he had ordered the U.S. Navy to "quarantine" Cuba. All ships headed for Cuba would be stopped and searched for missile parts and weapons. He also told Khrushchev to have his military take apart the missiles that were already in Cuba and immediately send them back to the Soviet Union.

The world waited, teetering on the edge of nuclear war. At least twenty-three Soviet ships were headed toward Cuba. The American military went into full alert. Long-range bombers, each carrying four H-bombs, took to the sky. The Russians took similar military actions. People around the world feared that these actions were more than saber-rattling.

U.S. Secretary of State Dean Rusk said to ambassadors, "I would not be candid and I would not be fair with you if I did not say we are in as grave a crisis as mankind has been in."[3] Doomsday might be only hours away.

Then, three days after Kennedy announced his quarantine, the Soviet ships sailing for Cuba stopped and turned around. Secretary of State Rusk said the situation was like two boys on the verge of a schoolyard fistfight. "We were eyeball to eyeball, and the other fellow just blinked."[4]

Talks between Americans and Russians took place in secret. The Soviet Union agreed to withdraw its missiles if the United States promised it would never invade Cuba. The United States promised to remove its intermediate-range missile base in Turkey, near the Soviet border.

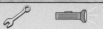
Banning Tests

The Cuban Missile Crisis was the most dramatic and dangerous moment of the Cold War. After the frightening showdown, both sides took steps toward peace.

In July 1963, the United States, the Soviet Union, and Great Britain agreed to stop atmospheric testing of atomic and hydrogen bombs. These tests had released dangerous poisons into the air over the years. Underground testing was allowed to continue.

In August 1963, the United States and the Soviet Union set up a "hot line," a direct telephone link between their headquarters. Better communications between the two sides might stop a nuclear war. Both countries feared that a nuclear war might start by accident.

Disagreements Among Friends

Alliances in both the Communist and non-Communist worlds began to crumble. Russia and China disagreed about the goals of true Communism. China was especially upset about Russia's warmer relations with the United States. Czechoslovakia tried to break away from the Eastern Bloc in 1968. However, Soviet-backed troops invaded and stopped the nation's move toward independence. There were problems in the Western alliance too. France rejected United States and British leadership and dropped out of NATO in 1967.

The Vietnam Conflict

In the late 1960s, the United States supported South Vietnam in its struggle with Communist North Vietnam. American involvement in Vietnam lasted from about 1965

CNN - Cold War - Microsoft Internet Explorer

File   Edit   View   Favorites   Tools   Help

Address 🔄 http://www.cnn.com/SPECIALS/cold.war/episodes/01/maps/

CNNiN
interactive
CNN.com

* CNN PERSPECTIVES SERIES
Available Now on Home Video

COLD WAR

Episode-by-Episode
Cold War Experience
  culture
  technology
  espionage
  the bomb
Knowledge Bank
Debate and Discuss
Cold War Challenge
Educator's Guide

About the Series
About the Site
Awards
Cold War Home Video

RESEARCH*it*

GO

Feedback ✉

EPISODE 1: COMRADES | INTERACTIVE MAP

OCCUPIED
GERMANY

SOVIET OCCUPIED
TERRITORY

| PREWAR-1939 | TURNING POINT-1943 | COLD WAR-1947 |

Cold War rivalries are already forming, just two
years after the end of World War II. The Soviet
Union, exhausted but triumphant after the
conflict, has taken control of Poland, Bulgaria,
Romania and Hungary. Czechoslovakia, recently

http://www.cnn.com/SPECIALS/cold.war/episodes/01/maps/#

Internet

This map shows Soviet-occupied and Communist territory as of 1947.
By 1949, it had spread into Asia, sparking conflicts such as the Korean
and Vietnam Wars.

through 1973. In those years approximately 58,000
Americans died in Vietnam.

American leaders entered this war because they feared
the "domino theory." This theory presumes that if one
nation falls to Communism, then—like a line of domi-
noes—other nations will also fall. The leaders of the
United States wanted to stop the fall of the first domino.

Millions of Americans, especially the young, opposed
the war. Antiwar riots broke out on college campuses.
Many young men refused to serve in the army. More than
any other event of the twentieth century, the Vietnam War
divided the nation.

Peaceful Competition

"**W**e will bury you," Nikita Khrushchev once warned the West. The Soviet leader was not talking about war. He believed the Communist countries would produce more radios, televisions, and refrigerators than the capitalist countries. They did not succeed. However, the Soviets won victories in other areas.

▶ The Space Race

On October 4, 1957, Americans received shocking news. A Russian object the size of a basketball was in orbit 100 miles or more above the earth. Impossible, cried Americans. The United States is the most technically advanced country in the world. *We* were supposed to launch the first satellite. Yet the satellite flew, and its name was *Sputnik*, Russian for "traveler."

The *Sputnik* satellite started the space race between the United States and the Soviet Union. The space race followed naturally from the arms race. Rockets that carried nuclear warheads could also launch space satellites.

The Americans lost the early stages of the space race. The nation's embarrassment grew as one United States rocket after another exploded on the launch pad. The first U.S. spacecraft, *Explorer I*, went into orbit on January 31, 1958. This was three months after the Russians sent up *Sputnik II*, which carried a dog named Laika.

In 1959, Russia's *Luna I* zoomed past the moon. On April 12, 1961, Russian Yuri Gagarin made a single orbit

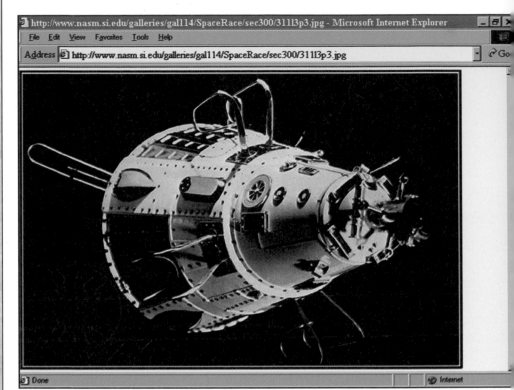

In 1958, just six months after it launched the first earth satellite, Sputnik, the Soviets put Sputnik II, pictured here, into orbit. The Soviet Union's lead in the space race infuriated the United States, who believed they were more technologically advanced.

around the earth. He became the first human in space. The Communists always seemed to be a step ahead.

Then, in the mid-1960s, the United States began to catch up. On July 20, 1969, American astronaut Neil Armstrong put the first human footprint on the moon.

The success of the United States in reaching the moon brought an end to the space race. As the Cold War became less tense, the United States and the Soviet Union even cooperated in space. In 1975, a three-man American spacecraft docked with a two-man Russian vehicle. The crew members shook hands and joked together.

▶ Sports

Usually, the Olympic games celebrate international friendship and peaceful competition between athletes. During the Cold War, however, each side tried to use the games to display its strength and superiority.

The Communist athletes included graceful female gymnasts. At Munich in 1972, the Russian gymnast Olga Korbut thrilled the world with her dazzling performances. The tiny Romanian Nadia Comaneci won two gold medals in the 1976 summer games in Montreal. Communist East Germany, a country with a population of only 17 million, won a total of forty gold medals in 1976. East German women swimmers were especially successful.

Excitement rose when United States and Russian teams competed against each other. In the 1960 Winter Olympics, the American hockey team faced a strong Russian team. The Russians took a 2–1 lead and seemed to be headed to victory. Then, the Americans fought back to win an amazing 3–2 upset.

In 1972, the United States lost a basketball competition to the Soviet Union. The American team refused to accept the silver medal for second place. The players believed they were cheated out of a victory. The American hockey team won another stunning upset at the 1980 winter games held in Lake Placid, New York.

Cold War squabbles broke out often. The United States refused to attend the 1980 summer games in Moscow because the Soviet Union had invaded Afghanistan a year earlier. In turn, the Soviet Union and several other Communist countries boycotted the 1984 summer games in Los Angeles. Athletes from both sides suffered because they could not compete in the events of their dreams.

Chapter 6

The Cold War Ends

The Cold War affected all the nations of the world, even those that were not directly involved in the conflict. On December 3, 1989, President George Bush said there was "virtually no problem in the world—and certainly no problem in Europe" that would not be helped by an improvement in the U.S.-Soviet relationship.[1] The Cold War did not end with a bang. International tensions eased gradually.

▶ The 1970s and 1980s

A spirit of détente existed between the United States and the Soviet Union during much of the 1970s. *Détente* is a French word meaning "relaxation." Disagreements about Berlin became less heated. Traffic between West Germany and West Berlin was allowed to move freely.

Toward the end of the 1970s, however, détente faded. A "New Cold War," as some writers called it, began. New tensions arose in 1979 when the Soviet Union sent tanks and troops into Afghanistan. The United States protested this action and demanded that the Soviet troops leave Afghanistan. Many Russian soldiers were killed and wounded in Afghanistan and many Russian people opposed the war. The Afghan War has been called "Russia's Vietnam."

For years, the United States was against allowing Communist China to join the United Nations (UN). In 1971, the United States finally dropped its objections, and China became a member of the UN. The next

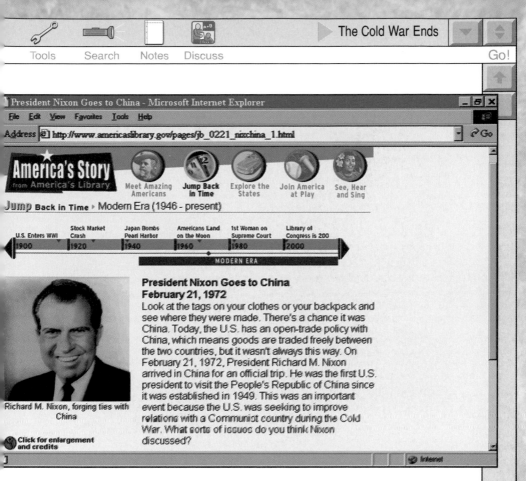

In 1972, President Richard Nixon became the first U.S. president to visit China since 1949. The purpose of the trip was to negotiate an open trade policy with Communist leader Mao Tse-Tung.

year, President Richard Nixon visited China. In 1979, the United States and China established formal diplomatic relations.

In the early 1970s, the United States and the Soviet Union worked to reduce nuclear weapons. President Nixon and Soviet leader Leonid Brezhnev signed the SALT I agreement in 1972. SALT stands for Strategic Arms Limitation Talks. Both sides agreed to limit their production of nuclear bombs.

Ronald Reagan was elected president in 1980 and the arms race took a new direction. Reagan once called

▲ *President Gerald R. Ford, left, and Premier Leonid Brezhnev, right, in a meeting in Vladivostok in November 1974.*

the Soviet Union an "evil empire." He greatly increased military spending. The Soviet Union tried to keep up with the American arms buildup but this effort weakened the Soviet economy.

Even so, Reagan enjoyed a warm friendship with Soviet leader Mikhail Gorbachev. The two men met several times, and in 1987, they agreed to destroy many of their ground-launched intercontinental missiles.

▶ Eastern Europe—A Bloc No More

During the 1980s, a labor union called Solidarity became powerful in Poland. That nation's ruling Communist Party was worried by its strength. At one point Solidarity was outlawed and its leader, Lech Walesa, was put in jail. Still, the union remained popular with the Polish people. In

1989, the union demanded free elections that included non-Communist candidates. Soon, candidates backed by Solidarity won the elections and Poland had a new, non-Communist government.

The rest of Eastern Europe watched the rise of democracy in Poland with great interest. A new spirit of freedom grew and could not be stopped. Soon Hungary, Czechoslovakia, and East Germany held free elections. They, too, threw out their Communist leaders.

▶ The Wall Comes Tumbling Down

On a clear night—November 11, 1989—crowds gathered on both sides of the Berlin Wall. Suddenly men and women began tearing down this symbol of oppression. No one ordered them to do this. Sledge hammers appeared out of nowhere. One by one, great sections of the hated wall came down. Cameras caught this magical moment on film. Berliners laughed and sang as they ripped apart the barrier that had divided their city for more than twenty-eight years. The nation of Germany was eventually reunited on October 3, 1990.

Historians view the destruction of the Berlin Wall as the official end of the Cold War. Today, pieces of the wall are sold as souvenirs of the Cold War era.

▶ The Soviet Union Falls as Well

Amazingly, the Communist Party in the Soviet Union lost control of the country in 1991. The Soviet Union, which was made up of fifteen republics (Russia being the largest), began to break up.

The collapse of Communism in Russia and Eastern Europe seemed to take place almost overnight. However, the Communist system had been losing strength for years.

http://americanhistory.si.edu/subs/history/timeline/end/images/inftreaty_full.jpg - Microsoft Internet Explo...

File   Edit   View   Favorites   Tools   Help

Address http://americanhistory.si.edu/subs/history/timeline/end/images/inftreaty_full.jpg

Done   Internet

▲ *In 1987, Soviet leader Mikhail Gorbachev, left, and President Ronald Reagan, right, signed the first agreement to destroy a whole class of nuclear weapons.*

Under Communism, a system of government offices—a *bureaucracy*—looks after the needs of the people. Bureaucracies move slowly. They do not adapt quickly to change. When a government cannot keep up with new developments, the people lose faith in their leaders and their system of government. Many observers say Communism was not destroyed. It simply collapsed.

▶ Old Friends and New

The Cold War lasted almost fifty years and kept the world in a state of fear. Although, with the exception of the

Korean and Vietnam Wars, it cost few lives. Still, it cost both sides fortunes, and left the economy of the former Soviet republics in poor shape. The shifts in political alliances during those fifty years show just how difficult international relationships can be.

By the year 2000, many of the former Soviet republics and the United States were becoming allies. Some have even suggested Russia, the strongest of the former republics, become a member of NATO. Although that may not happen, the Russians and Americans have been working together more closely.

When the United States was attacked by terrorists on September 11, 2001, the Russian government joined the United States in the war on terrorism. Russia even allowed American forces to use their military bases to launch attacks on the terrorist network in Afghanistan. When the two sides got together to negotiate over use of the bases, the Cold War seemed as if it were a distant memory.

Chapter 1. Drama in the Skies

1. David McCullough, *Truman* (New York: Simon & Schuster, 1992), p. 630.

Chapter 2. The Seeds of War

1. Martin Walker, *The Cold War: A History* (New York: Henry Holt and Company, 1993), p. 41.

Chapter 3. The 1950s: The Cold War at Home and Abroad

1. Harold Evans, *The American Century* (New York: Alfred A. Knopf, 2000), p. 402.

2. William Leuchtenburg, *The Age of Change* (Alexandria, Va.: Time-Life Books, 1977), pp. 54–55.

Chapter 4. The World at the Brink

1. Harold Evans, *The American Century* (New York: Alfred A. Knopf, 2000), p. 488.

2. Theodore Sorensen, *Kennedy* (New York: Harper & Row, 1965), p. 703.

3. Jeremy Isaacs, *The Cold War: An Illustrated History* (Boston: Little, Brown and Company, 1998), p. 195.

4. Martin Walker, *The Cold War: A History* (New York: Henry Holt and Company, 1993), p. 178.

Chapter 6. The Cold War Ends

1. Jeremy Isaacs, *The Cold War: An Illustrated History* (Boston: Little, Brown and Company, 1998), p. 394.

Further Reading

Collier, Christopher and James Lincoln Collier. *The United States in the Cold War.* Tarrytown, N.Y.: Marshall Cavendish Corporation, 2001.

Foster, Leila Merrell. *The Story of the Cold War.* Danbury, Conn.: Children's Press, 1990.

Heater, Derek B. *The Cold War.* Danbury, Conn.: Watts, Franklin, 1989.

Isaacs, Jeremy. *The Cold War: An Illustrated History.* Boston: Little, Brown and Company, 1998.

Jian, Chen. *Mao's China & the Cold War.* Chapel Hill: University of North Carolina Press, 2001.

Kort, Michael G. *The Cold War.* Brookfield, Conn.: Millbrook Press, Inc., 1994.

Mastny, Vojtech. *The Cold War and Soviet Insecurity: The Stalin Years.* New York: Oxford University Press, Inc., 1998.

McAleavy, Tony. *Superpower Rivalry: The Cold War, 1945–1991.* New York: Cambridge University Press, 1998.

McCullough, David. *Truman.* New York: Simon & Schuster, 1992.

Pietrusza, David. *The End of the Cold War.* Farmington Hills, Mich.: Gale Group, 1994.

Sherrow, Victoria. *Joseph McCarthy and the Cold War.* Farmington Hills, Mich.: Gale Group, 1998.

Speakman, Jay. *The Cold War.* Farmington Hills, Mich.: Gale Group, 2001.

Tusa, Ann and John Tusa. *The Berlin Airlift.* New York: Perseus Books Group, 1998.

Walker, Martin. *The Cold War: A History.* New York: Henry Holt and Company, 1993.

Warren, James A. *Cold War: The American Crusade Against the Soviet Union and World Communism, 1945–1990.* New York: HarperCollins Children's Book Group, 1996.